Cora

CORACLE

Poems by Kenneth Steven

First published in Great Britain in 2014

Society for Promoting Christian Knowledge
36 Causton Street
London SW1P 4ST
www.spckpublishing.co.uk

British Library Cataloguing-in-Publication Data
A catalogue record for this book is available from the British Library

ISBN 978-0-281-07209-5
eBook ISBN 978-0-281-07210-1

Typeset by Caroline Waldron, Wirral, Cheshire
First printed in Great Britain by Ashford Colour Press
Subsequently digitally printed in Great Britain

eBook by Graphicraft Limited, Hong Kong

Produced on paper from sustainable forests

For Kristina,
with love

Contents

Acknowledgements

Poems in this collection have previously appeared in the pages of the following outlets: *Acumen, Causeway, Coracle, The Countryman, The Eildon Tree, Envoi, The Herald* (Glasgow), *Life and Work, Northwords Now, Poetry Ireland Review, Poetry Scotland, Quadrant* (Australia), *Resurgence, Scintilla, The Scots Magazine* and *Temenos Academy Review*. 'The Words' was read on BBC Radio 4.

 CORACLE

A round of dryness, one man strong
Woven and stitched to bob
The slow fishponds and the deeper creeks,
The waterways of crannogs:

Out even to the up and down of sea,
The blue bell of water that does not end,
But reaches, by the compass of the stars –
Another island and a new beginning.

 IONA

And God said:
Let there be a place made of stone
Out off the west of the world,
Roughed nine months by gale,
Rattled in Atlantic swell.

A place that rouses each Easter
With soft blessings of flowers
And shocks of white shell sand;
A place found only sometimes
By those who have lost their way.

# CLOISTER

The garden is walled with quiet
Ten feet tall. I have come inside a silence.

Rose petals jewelled with dew
And in each one a sun.

Swallows, soft felt flittings, trapeze the air;
An endless whisper of criss-crossings.

I hear a woven hum of bees
Holding their notes, hovering, burrowing deep,

As the sun unsmudges from the mist
And morning, warm, in blue and gold, begins.

 THE WORDS

All night I wrestled with an angel, sure
He carried words that I must make my own.
Hour after hour I fought and cried because I could not win,
Because I feared those words would die unknown.

And by the time this morning bled the skies
I'd neither won nor lost, but I could fight no more;
As that first fire of light began to rise

I turned, went out, barefoot, into the dawn
Empty of everything and heard the choir of birds,
And all at once I knew what I should write –
They came alive, they grew – these were my words.

# A GREEN WOODPECKER

The day is like dead wood –
No colours, only shades of grey.

The gentle breath of my steps
Leaves a ghost story written in the grass.

A stillness like that when snow falls
Except there is no snow, and none all winter –

Only the river in its silvering among the trees
Whispers the same old journey to the sea;

Only the moon, low above the hills,
Frail as a ball of cobwebs.

On moss feet, I go into the wood
And a great door closes behind me:

Little quiverings of things
Quick among twigs;

Two deer, their eyes listening,
Flow into nowhere in a single blink.

I look up, into a pool of light
And hold my breath:

Swans stretching north
Swimming the open sky –

The silence so huge
I hear their wings.

And I think,
As I begin to go back home;

I came here searching one bird
And found all this instead:

How like my life.

 # AFTER THE STORM

The valley lay in the window
Dazed and damaged.

The river horsed under bridges
Swirling with earth and rain.

The fields were filled with mirrors, glass stretches
Reflecting a breaking sky.

The house was silent, left unhumming –
We were powerless; there was nothing we could do.

GEORGE

It was after a gas attack he found the bird
And brought it back still warm in those big hands.

A lark he said it was. They agreed, later on that night,
Poking fun at him still crouching there, feeding the thing

Bits of cheese and worms grubbed up from mud.
He'd always been the odd one out, not one of them:

Got yourself a bird at last, George! they sniggered,
Told him it was probably a German spy,

Would be off back over to their lines
Soon as it had word of the next offensive.

He didn't care. It held him, gave him something back
Of Dartmoor, those days with his Dad up on the tors

In the early summer winds. How the larks rose
Twirling songs until you lost them in the sunlight;

How they'd watch them rise and rise as if on strings
Till all the sky seemed full of them.

He didn't give a fig for cards, never heeded all the jibes
As night boomed huge and strange about them.

Was a sniper picked him off on sentry duty, though –
Probably when he was far off in his thoughts

Back on the moors of home and walking miles and miles.
A single bullet through the head and he was gone.

They clasped the bird into his hands (who the hell
Was going to go on feeding it when he was dead?)

And that night there was a quiet in the place,
A strangeness, something that wasn't there.

 # HORSES

Since back before the world
Began becoming small –
We knew them. How long
To learn to break them
Into furrows, into the first fields?

Yet when they were born
Such things on stilts, longer than possible,
All snort and struggle, floundering
In the wet morning upwards
Into themselves, that first stand.

Strange the soft invisible cord
Threading child and horse together
In the dark dawn of the stable;
Words fed like warm hay
Gentling fear, readying the journey.

Not broken, bonded.
They were themselves always;
Running the sudden sun
Of a field's lit green –
Only because it was there.

We folded them with reverence
Back into warm loam
That had borne them.
They gave us beauty
Out of our brute beginnings.

 CALVINISM

A layer of rock
That grows no trees. Out of it
Hills guilty of no sin
Keep their old heads bowed.

Here is a religion
Made of what may not be done;
Its wood and nails have turned
To stone much sterner than its maker.

Yet ask for help on some November night
And a door will open
On kindness precious and without price –
As old as the one from Galilee.

 EASTER LILIES

We forget all about them
In the year's darkness, in the long winter

Without a sound they are there one morning
A kind of sunlight grown from the ground

As if some call had woken them
From the underworld of their sleep

Out into the middle of March
To Easter the earth with their heads

Flapped and flayed by the wind
Broken yolks splashing the air

All that we had hoped for
An answer to prayer

# SCHOOL

Wooden desks on metal legs
Inkwells in them still;
Windows stretching high and empty,
Scuffing feet on stairs.

Each day and every day
The slow march of clocks' hands,
Until the last long shrill bell –
Fractions and maths all rubbed to dust.

Sometimes I took a note along a corridor,
On padded feet past windowed doors;
The sadness of Latin nouns being chanted,
The thrashing of the belt, the sound of stillness.

Bullying happened in other schools, not ours;
Kicks came cleverly in dark places, round the back
Of buildings out of sight. Nonetheless,
It was the cuts inside that hurt the worst.

Now, twenty-five years further on,
I touch and hear and feel it all the same.
School fits in a smaller and smaller bag
At the back of an old cupboard in the attic –

But I can't get rid of it, I never will.

PATIENT

Even the grass and the trees seem sick,
Afraid of what might happen around the next
Corner. Corridors smell of shouting and tears;
The windows are huge opportunities
For suicide. You listen constantly for silence,
Your eyes always looking for trouble,
The long miles inside your mind
Sleepless with ghosts. I talk in small pieces
About home, Yugoslavia, summer,
The amazing speed of years –
And want away, out of this place's illness.
I go gratefully, mad to reach
The wide blue skies of the world outside,
Clutching at the wildest hope
That one day you might leave
The other self that haunts you here behind –
Its leprous, terrible hide –
Break back into the beautiful, smooth skin of childhood
And come back home.

# PUNISHMENT

The sun had been wet for days,
Raining light across the city.
That day it broke through
So all was glass –
Fragments of shattered glass.

I am putting myself together
Piece by piece. I cannot see myself
In a mirror yet. I was going home
At five o'clock, was hurrying
To find a present for my daughter.

Now there's too much time;
Every day's so big, so far too big.
I look out the window and watch
Children catching laughter in the lane,
So bright and still unbroken.

I don't know where he came from:
Everything happened so fast,
Will last for ever.
He got nine years –
I was given life.

 A KIND OF COMING BACK

Sometimes I imagine the phone ringing in the night –
That worst of all nightmares – and staggering out
Into the darkness of the hall. My small voice
Asking the question – afraid, white, far away –
My father answering, ten years dead, as though
Nothing at all had happened. Asking me how I am
As in the old days, when I came home from university,
When he put down his pen in the study and turned
That half-smile on his face. *I'm fine*
I whisper now, ghostly, into the nothingness of the night –
Knowing this cannot be, this is impossible.
I'm glad, he says, serious at last, as though he means it,
And puts the phone down, leaving the humming nothing
Of that no man's land between the worlds.

 PEARS

I think of that house in early evening
Somewhere at the end of summer

All the doors and windows open
Filled with the afterglow of sun

And the whole house heavy with the scent of pears.
There in the lawn that ancient tree

A hundred summers old, and maybe more,
Around it a deep, dark ring of pears.

I picked them hour after long hour
To thud into baskets, heavy and melting –

Leaving only the broken ones,
All drizzled and wandering with wasps,

And it was as if the house became some strange ship
I was filling for a long voyage

That the rest of our lives might be made of pears.

 MOONS

A ball of ice in the May skies
Grazed by its old seas, riding
Like a glass balloon above the moors.

Underneath, the moon of Scotland
A bald skull long north
Clicked alone by flint stags.

Both moons kingless tonight
Silent of voice and all lost
Dead in the skies of history.

 OTTER

light swivels on the night's edge:
the full moon's eerie beam
wobbles like a child's balloon, huge, and breaks
upwards at last, into the clearing dark

otter trundles over wetscapes, crying
as points of mild-white stars shine clear;
he curls into himself in seaweed
through the swell and ebb of tide until
the oystercatchers drip their calls across the sky
and orange-gold the dark melts into day –
then he's off, a scamper on the sea edge
scenting, searching, circling –
flowing into river edges, a thousand streams
sewn inside the silk of him, for ever

 # THE MID-MARCH FROGS

The hills were low and furry;
We curved the hill road, into the warm dark,
Saying things in snatches, wrapped in night wool.
Out of our headlights the frozen ghost of an owl,
Was gone.

We saw the frogs gradually –
They grew into shadows out of the road's soft stone.
We slowed to a hum, leaned forwards to watch them;
They were luminous and rubbery,
Some with one webbed hand raised, but all listening:
Heads held erect, hearing some ancient song,
Something that had called them into this strange river
In the sudden jolt of spring.

We edged the car round them, slow as a cyclist
Might wobble his way between walls.
And we thought with agony
Of the other cars that would come
Through the long shadow of that night,
Over the hill to the other side, slushing senselessly,
Leaving imprints of frogs, frog rubbings,
Written there like cave paintings, thin as skin.

 TED

Once a week he came for dinner
When I was four or five.

Long afterwards I learned
He'd fought in the First World War.

Back then the only thing I cared about
Was the bar of chocolate that he brought me.

I thanked him,
Then ran off to bed.

He was dead
Before I'd even gone to school.

If there were picks and shovels
That could dig a tunnel down through time

To break out in that house again
And find those nights, I'd go –

To sit with him and ask
What he'd brought back, what he remembered,

Not like some bounty hunter after sparkling things
To shove in pockets, show off and sell,

But quiet, listening, hungering to understand
The truth of how it was out there,

To look through his old eyes and see
The shattered fragments of those years,

To piece together shard by shard
A little of the story that was his:

That place, that price.

 LAPWINGS

Once upon a time they came in clouds
To dip and swivel over opened fields;

The spring wind, patched with sunlight,
And lapwings up above and all around –

A shimmer of iridescent green.
Now there are no more.

I hear their absence, waken in the early light
Knowing they are gone and won't return.

I watch for them still, wishful,
But all the fields are bare and silent.

We called them peewits, the name made
To try to catch that sweep of soft call

And we heard a hundred all at once
They wove into one another, made a knot

As if from cotton, soft, across the skies.
I'll keep that safe, somewhere inside my head.

But what will I tell my child happened to the lapwings?

 FINLAGGAN

It was a day in late October. All night the rain
Had chattered Gaelic round the house.

We drove through sheets of water
Skies tugging with the wind –

Up to the north-east of the island,
The last miles of Islay.

At Finlaggan we thudded the doors shut,
Went out under wet skies.

And the man in the museum came to meet us,
Came hurrying over full of sorries.

For the walkway to the island had flooded,
There was no way we'd get there;

He read our disappointment,
Heard it in our silence.

I'll carry you out, he decided –
I'll carry you to the other side.

And he did. He waded the black water
That swirled above his knees:

Four times he went through,
Back and forth, back and forth –

Left us over on the island,
Promised he'd bring us back in an hour.

On that day of greyness
I looked all around –

Not a light on the desolate moors.
And I thought of Scotland then:

Hundreds of miles of silence,
Hundreds of years ago –

A nameless place, an uncrowned kingdom,
And thought how once upon a time

Here at Finlaggan,
In the high days of the chiefs –

The banquets and the battles,
Nights of story and of song –

They had to be carried across
To reach the island dryshod.

 LEAVING THE ISLAND

The day windless and pale;
The hills rubbed out with mist.
Donald Angus leaves a note in English on the mantel,
Each word chiselled slow and beautiful in ink.
The dogs drowned obedient in the bay;
The men come wordless back, the hands at their sides hurt.
They help the eldest down the long steps;
She murmurs Gaelic, soft sounds that make no longer any
                                                    sense.
They go onto the ship, their blue eyes flickering about them –
Out on the water, the psalm lifts – a great and rising wave.

A mainland that was out of sight
Has grown clearer and clearer,
Glints now on the horizon, made of sugar and tobacco –
Of everything that they have missed too long.

Yet this life is in the beat of the blood,
Is written in their hands as sore as salt;
What can they do but climb cliffs, net birds, build stone –
They're worthless in a world that's made of talk.
In their language there are no words for theft or envy,
They have only songs for when the darkness falls.

In all the cobbled, concrete years to come
Their island promises to lie at the bottom of a glass,
Or silent for ever in their eyes, a story frozen
Like a fly in the amber of time.

 AFTER ALL

It wasn't for the Greek and Hebrew that he quoted,
that meant no more than the city he had come from,
with a wife scared of horses, who couldn't gut a rabbit.
It wasn't for the ramblings of sermons, wild as ivy,
that lost them long before the end,
that had them yearning out of unstained windows
at the bright-swept springtime light, the newborn fields.

No, it was rather for the steps he climbed
unseen and quiet, for the bread of words he broke
to feed a dying soul, the midnights that he trudged
the hillside of a man who'd lost his child
and could not sleep for grieving. It was for that
beneath the hurrying skies that late November day
they came bareheaded down the lanes to say farewell.

 GLENLYON

All January the hills curved with perfect snow;
Now this morning the grazed eyeball of a moon
Rolls into blue silence. A sunlight,
Frail and liquid, sluices all the fields.

A tattered huddle of a lamb
Rends the day with sadness.
The trees whisper, lift and fall;
There flutters on the breeze sleet, soft as wool.

 GLENDALOUGH

The ghost of the mist lifting
From a sea folding over in silk.

In the night a flicker of snow,
The final breathing of winter –

But down in the nooks of the rocks
Yellow petals and bright spires.

In darkness the monk comes out
Soundless from the cell where he sleeps

Crouches in the lee of the boulders,
Holds open the bowl of his hands

So deep and nestled in prayer
He never knows the blackbird's circling

And when he wakens from the world of his God,
The day fierce with the spines of the sunlight

She lies warm in his woven fingers
The eggs kept there under her softness.

How long he held there who knows,
For the story is older than stone

But the annals say that he waited
Till the young birds flew up to the sky –

And if the shards of the telling are true
And the rest just the spinning of legend

It is bigger than we can believe.

 # THE GHOST ORCHID

One day, when the air is sore to breathe
And the seas are dead and heavy, thudding
Over empty shores, and only a dwindling of us

Remain – strange, in hiding,
From yellow and red skies,
From scabbed earth –

We will draw in caves
The eerie shapes
Of everything we remember;

We will weave out of firelight
What fields meant, what horses were,
The story of flowing water, of birds bringing morning into
song.

And for a while
Before we have grown old
Like moss on rocks, furred and searching with age,

Our children will believe
It was that beautiful,
That good.

 # THE UNFOUND

Every spring we head out there
To the ploughed fields of Fife,
Beneath the greylag geese
And flocks of snow that billow east.

All his life he wanted to compose;
Music's still alive inside his fingers,
But everything he's ever written
Has been neglected, and he knows it.

We walk the ploughed fields hour by hour
For lumps of stone like old potatoes,
Clagged with mud and heavy as clenched fists;
Their secrets sleeping deep inside.

Yet when they're split they're made of rings
Like slices of a fossil tree, and coloured
Ochre, silver, dragon blue and red –
And no two agates ever quite the same.

It's when I leave I think
Perhaps the best are left behind
Unfound, unopened where they lie,
And all they might have been unknown.

 # TWO WRENS DEAD

Fifteen below.
A whole foot of snow
Crystalled and glinting.

All winter eight of them, snub-tailed,
Inch in under the eaves,
Cuddle against the cold.

This winter just too big –
Day after day of deep ice,
The sky made of strange marble.

I found them. Beaks like twigs:
Eyes glazed and gone,
Their light put out for ever.

How little did they weigh,
And yet, all day I held them
Heavy in my heart.

 DAFYDD

A guesthouse in Belfast;
The shyness of a shared table.
The man who's there already's Welsh –
From North Wales, the real Wales.
Tea and bacon and eggs and toast.
Now in my head I'm back on Anglesey
Among the few good friends I made on two short stays.
I fish their names from half-forgotten shadows;
Names not thought of long enough. I hear voices,
Remember nights of song and walks on windy shores.
Then there's someone else, someone I knew in Scotland –
Someone who'd been friends with R. S. Thomas.
Dafydd, I begin, *Dafydd Owen*!
And this man's eyes begin to fill with tears –
I worked ten years with Dafydd, he says –
And we sit there, having found the link, the piece between us.
I think of Dafydd: vibrant, wild and fiery,
Generous-hearted, eyes that danced with talk and laughter;
Dafydd who died of cancer way before his time.
There in Belfast we talk of him
Like two men beside a bonfire, lit by the strange flames
Of someone who's resurrected by such talk –
Who's there again in front of us, as large as life.

 THE PLACE WHERE RIVERS MEET

The place where rivers meet the Celts believed was sacred;
They built chapels there and buried precious things.

One day in mid-July I go down where there is no path,
Breaking my way like a bear

As the sun flutters
Through the green flickering of the trees.

I stop and listen, hold my breath,
Sweat thick across my forehead and my eyes.

The water is so low it only slides, searches in among the rocks;
Sifting its slow journey to the sea:

No birds, no beasts, only the clear flashes of the sun,
Light dancing in the glades.

And then I break out on the beach,
That place where two rivers mingle.

I stand there thinking of who was there before me,
Of what might be beneath my feet.

I take my shoes off in case the place is holy,
Swirl them in the lukewarm of the water –

And sing something soft, a long time.

 EDITH

Her son was dying, lay at the end of a disease
On a machine, unable to move any more,
A ghost of his old self – in the blink of a year
After first falling ill.

Yet he never made any complaint,
Just kept on fighting to breathe
For the two little faces who came to his bedside
He would never see run or play.

She had lost God a long time ago, she said.
And what did I have to give her?
I felt like a dry well, hollow and empty –
Nothing but the same old echoes.

She looked at me, her face bewildered with grief;
Her eyes met mine as she said:
It's not how you live your life,
But how you go to the gallows.

 THE CHAPEL

A woman will come on a ragged day
Of swaying wind and rain,
Up a road unmetalled, almost washed away –
Held against her breast a child,
Brittle and yellowed, its cries like a kitten's,
And her gentled hand softening its sorrow.

Here, to this ancient sanctuary on the hill,
A shelter now for sheep,
Through the thick smothering of winter snows;
A place broken by emptiness, its door blown in –
And the woman, her hands full of cold,
Will splash some water in the font
And draw it long across her child's head,
Mumbling the memory of some words
Her mother might have heard.

 SON

He grabbed a lunchbox and his bag
and banged the door;
she tried to call but he was gone –
his fifty pence forgotten.

It lies there still.
Outside, the city morning rushes past;
the house has fallen quiet, empty –
she sits and waits and watches.

She's cut the seconds up,
to sift and piece them one by one:
the frames, the sounds, the single beats –
they lie in piles across the floor.

He ran across the road,
turned once to wave, and there's his face –
the photograph of how he froze
a blink before the car.

That single frame of him turned round and smiling
above the mantelpiece, out in the hall,
upstairs on every bedroom wall – his picture
always saying goodbye.

This is her waiting room,
the place she comes to sit so patient,
where she has nothing left to do
but watch the clock push back the time of day.

# RUANAN

I am the limping one,
Born with a broken foot that dragged me through
The bullying of school,
The rough and tumble of this world.

I came here because they did not judge;
They said they wanted my soft voice for song,
They loved me for the raw and rough-hewn thing I was,
And did not shape me for their ends.

It is my task to bring water from the well
For the monastery, each dawn. Sometimes
The sore of frost beneath bare feet,
The salt sprinkle of the stars above.

Every time I draw that heavy dark aloft
I think of how the Master asked to drink,
Asked to drink of the water from the well,
And it's for him I limp back in the darkness every dawn.

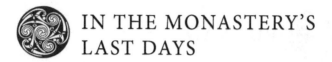# IN THE MONASTERY'S
LAST DAYS

the stained glass window
that has been the sun fails
and these hands slow and steady fall

outside the winter; the frail light
pales the valley one more moment as his grey eyes
remember all this place has been

through forty years of stone, knelt prayer and song
all passed now, and he
leaving for a world he has forgotten,
has not thought of for so long

what will he make now of the dawn, of noon or evensong
when there are none to mark the day with him

he will find those hours alone
until he is called back home at last
and makes that final walk, glad
hands empty and yet full of light.

 HALLOWE'EN

a gloved moon
in the sky's thickness

the smell of everything
blown down by gales

children wrapped as ghosts
knocking at lit doors

for shiver-red apples
and a bronze scatter of coins

by midnight
the moon the eye of an old man

looking through a keyhole
grazed and ancient

and the village asleep
under a woollen blanket of mist

 DEFINING AN ISLAND

It's more than just land
Surrounded by sea. There's a hold on all that lives
That's stronger here. Look at the windswept children
Scurrying the lane to school; they grow up learning
The carrying of lambs and the bringing in of boats.
Don't romance them. Their parents have turned hard
From all the northerlies that came to shake the place
Like a terrier a rat. They'll gut a fish
And wipe both blood and gills on old towel
Without a word. But when the youngest son drowns
At the lobsters, or far out in the fishing grounds,
They're not afraid to let the waves go through them,
To show their anger at the sea in grief
That's big and sore. It's a long winter here,
Most of it spent remembering. That's what whisky's for.

 WAY OUT WEST

It will always be this way –
So loud with the tugging of the Atlantic
Only a few will live here,
Chimneys gusting heathery smoke.

Words are not wasted,
And answers carved out of granite;
They lean against the wind, faces
Ledged with storm, with high tides.

Around their crofts, dead tractors and machinery
Turn the colour of bracken in autumn.
Collie dogs lie blown out in the wind
With eyes like lochs.

But on a Saturday night
The windows are honeyed with light,
A fiddle bends tunes from thin air
And songs stretch far into morning.

 ENOUGH

Out of the scurry of the days
A place of late sunlight, and the sky
Swimming into blue unclouded;
The trees held in a bonfire of the last sun.

Enough to wait here by the wood's edge
And let the things still hurrying to be done
Fall silent, as the first stars
Vague the orange of the far-off west.

# THE HERMIT'S CELL

To Ali

I had to listen for a silence
that was born inside.
It took a whole year to find
and now it does not fail.

I need nothing;
all I want is where I am.

I used to pray, and praying then
was struggle with myself.
Now I am made prayer, am hollowed out –
a song that needs no sound.

I pick the blow of flowers, bring them back
in blues and reds and golds,
and in the slow of winter dark
I watch for dawn and know
that I am growing into light
a little every day.